THE BATTLE
OF BRITAIN
MEMORIAL
FLIGHT

First published in the UK in 2000
by Airlife Publishing Ltd

British Library Cataloguing-in-Publication Data
    A catalogue record for this book
    is available from the British Library

ISBN 1 84037 200 1

Typeset by Rowland Phototypesetting Ltd,
Bury St Edmunds, Suffolk
Printed in Italy

Airlife Publishing Ltd

101 Longden Road, Shrewsbury, SY3 9EB, England
E-mail: airlife@airlifebooks.com
Website: www.airlifebooks.com

THE BATTLE OF BRITAIN MEMORIAL FLIGHT

Martin W. Bowman

Airlife
England

THE DEBT WE OWE

To the 70,253 RAF aircrew (of whom 47,293 were from Bomber Command) lost on operations 3 September 1939 to 14 August 1945. And to the 2,945 pilots and aircrew (of whom 507 were KIA, and 500 wounded) who flew operationally under Fighter Command control in the Battle of Britain, 10 July to 31 October 1940.

'The gratitude of every home in our island, in our Empire and, indeed, through the world, except in the abodes of the guilty, goes out to the British airmen, who, undaunted by odds, unweary in their constant challenge and mortal danger, are turning the tide of the world war by their prowess and their devotion. Never in the field of human conflict was so much owed by so many to so few.'

Winston S. Churchill, 20 August 1940

CONTENTS

ROLL THE CREDITS

Camera Ship pilot ..... Dale Featherby
Camera ships courtesy ..... Mark Shaw
Focus puller/key grip/tail gunner ..... Yours truly
Pilots ..... Grp Capt Peter Ruddock
..... Grp Capt Al Lockwood AFC
..... Wg Cdr Dave Harrison
..... Wg Cdr Nick Watson
..... Sqn Ldr Paul Day OBE AFC
..... Sqn Ldr 'Shiney' Simmons
..... Sqn Ldr Dave Buchanan
..... Sqn Ldr Clive Rowley
..... Sqn Ldr Dave Thomas
..... Flt Lt Giles 'Grubsy' Smerdon
..... Flt Lt Rolly Hendry
..... Flt Lt Merv Counter
Navigation ..... Sqn Ldr Brian Clark
..... Sqn Ldr Andy Marson
..... Flt Lt Garry Simm
..... Flt Lt Tony Dixon RAF (retd)
..... Sqn Ldr Paul 'Wilky' Wilkins
Air Engineers ..... WO Phil McConville
..... Sgt 'Ernie' Wise
2nd unit cameraman/
airframe technician/tail gunner ..... Chief Tech John 'Sid' Siddell
All other ranks ..... unsung heroes too numerous to mention
Safety equipment ..... Cpl Nick Timewell
Poets ..... Audrey Grealy
..... Jasper Miles
..... the late A. Burford Sleep
Chief strapper-ins/camera ship support ..... Dave 'Pedo' Puleston
..... Graeme 'Magoo' Tacon
Ops and Administration ..... Trace Wright
Adjutant and Operations Officer ..... Jack Hawkins
Hospitality ..... Janet Marshall
M/T driver ..... Paul Wilson
Public Relations ..... Dale Donovan RAF Strike Command PR
Special thanks to ..... Frank Mouritz RAAF (retd)
..... Kay Mason
..... Karen Wilsher of the Shuttleworth Trust
..... Touch Down Aero Centre
..... the late General Gord Ockendon DFC CD RCAF
..... Grp Capt Dave Seward AFC RAF (retd)
..... Peter R. Arnold
Cameras and lenses ..... Canon EOS
..... Jessops
Film stock ..... Fuji Sensia & Velvia transparency and Kodak and Fuji print
Film Processing ..... Reflections
Best boy ..... FIDO

All photographs by the author, unless otherwise acknowledged.

A MAJOR ROLE

'This story shall the good man teach his son:
We few, we happy few, we band of brothers.'
– *Henry V*, Act IV, Scene III by William Shakespeare

After his initial training at South Cerney in December 1961, Paul Day began his flying training at Syerston on the Jet Provost T.3 and T.4, progressing on to the Vampire T.11 at Swinderby, before beginning his operational career on the Hawker Hunter at 229 OCU, Chivenor, in November 1963. During his four tours he amassed 2,000 hours on the Hunter F.6, T.7, FGA.9 and FR.10, in Bahrain, Singapore and the UK. He converted to the F-4 Phantom at 228 OCU at Coningsby, and flew further tours in Germany, the USA and UK, achieving 3,000 hours on the F-4. While on an exchange tour with the USAF in Arizona, he acquired his nickname, the 'Major', as the USAF has no equivalent to the rank of Sqn Ldr. Returning to Coningsby in 1979, 'Major' resumed instructional duties on the Phantom. He converted to the

Déjà vu. *Hurricanes MK IIC PZ865 (nearest camera), flown by Wg Cdr Nick Watson, OC Operations Wing, and LF363, flown by Grp Capt Peter Ruddock, RAF Coningsby Station Commander, in the vicinity of RAF Wittering, where, on 11 September 1991, Sqn Ldr Allan 'Slam' Martin, put LF363 down after the engine started running rough, pouring smoke from all twelve exhaust stubs. The engine failed completely, resulting in a crash-landing on the airfield. Martin suffered some burns and a broken ankle as he scrambled away from the fierce fire which engulfed the Hurricane. This was the first air-to-air picture of the two Hurricanes together since LF363 rejoined the Flight in September 1998 after a total rebuild.*

Sortie completed, Grp Capt Peter Ruddock banks away from the Yak-52 camera ship.

Tornado F.3 in December 1988 and has 1,000 hours on type.

It was while flying the Phantom at Coningsby that Paul Day began his association with the BBMF, joining the Flight in 1980. Being the first non-piston-trained pilot to serve the BBMF, he was converted via the de Havilland Chipmunk, and then flew his first two seasons on the Hurricanes. 'Major' retraced his early BBMF career in 'A [Spitfire Pilot] Novice's Viewpoint' in a 1986 issue of Wingspan magazine, which is condensed here. At the time he was an air combat instructor with 228

OCU at Coningsby, a qualified weapons instructor (ground attack) on the Hunter and Phantom, and had logged more than 4,300 flying hours.

'I know that I was a Philistine. Eight years on ground-attack Hunters had left me with the opinion that if you weren't single-seat, 600 knots and never above 1,000 feet you were sub-human. A further eight years on strike-attack Phantoms mellowed that viewpoint; add another seat and another 100 knots, otherwise, no change. Thus, mentally crippled, I arrived back at Coningsby from a Phantom exchange posting in

Arizona – via a short brush with a ground tour – in 1979.

'As I started work with 228 (Phantom) OCU I barely noticed the co-located Spitfire/Hurricane operations, except as a nuisance which frequently got in the way of "real" aeroplanes. However, in late 1979 fate intervened. I was at a station commander's cocktail party where that worthy opined, with a distinctly military inflection, that I should "volunteer" for BBMF fighters and that my then boss, John Allison, fully supported the idea. Fearing more dire alternatives I duly acceded to the Vintage Mafia.

The Flight's finest hour? Sqn Ldr Paul Day leads his flock over Lincolnshire. The 'Major' took command from Sqn Ldr Rick Groombridge in April 1996, while retaining the additional role of Fighter Leader. In 1999 Paul Day was awarded the OBE in the Queen's Birthday Honours List. On 21 July 1999 the 'Major' achieved 1,000 hours flying Spitfires at the controls of PM631 in transit to a flypast at Mountbatten, near Plymouth, accompanied by RAF Coningsby station commander Grp Capt Peter Ruddock, who was flying Spitfire IIA P7350. The year 2000 is Sqn Ldr Day's twentieth season with the BBMF and he will remain at the helm for the first four years of the Millennium.

'On 14 May 1980 I presented myself to the Air Experience Flight at RAF Newton, resplendent in a flying-jacket advertising many thousands of heavy-metal hours, to bring the lowly Chipmunk to heel; this never struck me as being a problem despite never having touched any sort of piston. Things went wonderfully through the take-off, aerobatics, stalls and spins dutifully confirming the jet-age image. And then we started the

attempts to land. ATC clearly thought that the first half-dozen were a put-on, but then began to phone around the station to invite people to the tower balcony to watch the fun. The circuit emptied and I was left, centre stage, to do my worst. It took about an hour to demonstrate every conceivable way to leave a runway, at the end of which my instructor performed a perfect three-pointer, thanked me for the cabaret, and went to tea.

'Self-doubt is not in the fighter pilot's inventory, but that evening rocked my conviction that any aircraft would handle like an F-4. The next morning it clicked (to the dismay of the assembled punters) and I subsequently got through the Harvard with little drama, perhaps due to a more respectful approach – no pun intended. July 1980 was spent consolidating on the Chipmunk, and by the end of the month I had flown the Hurricane to display standard

Sqn Ldr Paul Day OBE AFC in the cockpit of Hurricane IIC PZ865.

and learned another valuable lesson about big pistons.

'First solo in the Hurricane took place on a beautiful day of the sort which makes you want to throw it about a bit, and so, straight and level at 2,000 feet, I mindlessly entered what I thought would be rapid aileron roll. Now, the Hurri's ailerons are not stunningly responsive, it turned out, and as I approached the inverted there was an awful lot of Lincolnshire and precious little sky in the window. This was resolved à la jet fighter by pushing the stick forward – only to be reminded that BBMF fighters, not being equipped with negative-G fuel systems, are a

bit prone to Merlin cough! Like self-doubt, panic is not in the inventory, but that roll was completed forty degrees nose down at 1,200 feet with rapid application of everything available. However, evidence was accruing that the "treat it like any other aircraft" syndrome needed modification. Thus, sparsely equipped, I started the Hurri for my first public display, at Newcastle on 31 July 1980 – quite a long way with no radio, but otherwise uneventful.

'Due to policy and a shortage of Spitfires available for conversion, it was not to be until May of 1982 that I got my hands on a Spit. Meanwhile, I determined to fly the Hurricane in a

manner so as to outshine the Spit, a task in which, no doubt, I singularly failed, but had much fun attempting. I also continued to investigate the pitfalls of historic aviation. I am frequently asked about the differences between flying the F-4 and the Spit or Hurri, the general assumption being that the Phantom must present the greater problem due to its size, Warp-9 capability, etc. Given that all aeroplanes bite fools, the reality is that the safer bet is the one to which the pilot is most accustomed – in my case the F-4 – and that the relatively unfamiliar Spit and Hurri should demand the maximum attention. And that is rightly so, but the excessive performance differences can open up avenues for complacency and subsequent embarrassment.

'On 21 September 1980 I took off in a Hurri with a Spitfire on each wing to do a flypast at RAF Wattisham, which was a low-key, in-house affair, followed by an important venue at RAF Staff College, Bracknell, landing at Biggin Hill. In addition, it had been agreed to make an airborne rendezvous over Wattisham with Richard Winslade to do air-to-air photography. The weather was CAVOK (ceiling and visibility OK), no navigational problems with crosswinds – BBMF aircraft have the original instrument fit – and no ATC problems until we entered the London CTZ for Bracknell. How, therefore, can a pilot with "n" hours in an F-4 in poor visibility in the German Low Flying system fail to find an airfield the size of Wattisham? It's easy. You note the passage of the first few features on the time and track, get ho-hum about the snail's pace 150 knots and, hey presto, look down and positively identify Bury St Edmunds as Newmarket. Puzzlement ensues, and there was puzzlement on the faces of the go-kart enthusiasts whose disused airfield we overflew in perfect formation, no doubt close to Wattisham; puzzlement turning to anger in Mr Winslade's voice as the certainty of an expensive missed RV developed; puzzlement mixed with disbelief in the controller's voice at Wattisham. I found that it concentrated my mind wonderfully against the immediate background of this lash-up to realise the consequences of

Winter Warm-up. Hurricane IIC PZ865 pictured running up its Merlin engine at RAF Coningsby.

Airborne again. PZ865, flown by Wg Cdr Nick Watson, OC Operations Wing, and LF363 US-C, flown by Grp Capt Peter Ruddock, RAF Coningsby Station Commander.

a similar performance before the jury of my peers at the much more difficult Bracknell venue. Fortunately, I got my ducks in a straighter line, but from that moment never again allowed myself to let go of the navigation.

'And so, deeply indebted to the Hurricane for a sound foundation in big-piston operations, I came to the Spitfire [AB910] on 5 May 1982. It would be dishonest to claim not to have lusted after the Spitfire ever since my enlightenment to "real" aeroplanes on joining BBMF in 1980,

and I see it as no disrespect to the Hurricane, which cannot be deprived of its place as having shouldered the brunt of the Battle of Britain, and gone on to be the fighter workhorse of the RAF in World War Two. And yet, the Hurricane displays its 1930s antecedence: chunky, thick-winged and rugged; canvas from the cockpit to tail; all of this combined to endow a multi-role capability, extreme ease of maintenance, relatively vice-free operation. And yet. The Spitfire, like Georgian silver or a best London gun, is one of those few artefacts which

one knows to be instinctively "right", and that knowledge in no way relies upon the professional expertise of the beholder. That may explain the Spit's continuing to be held in a special awe, almost reverence, by generations to whom the emotional attachments cannot apply. At its most base it is, undoubtedly, the second finest collection of geometric curves ever assembled; at best, one of the few examples of something which exceeds its aura and mystique in every way.

'Conversion to the Spit, while not

The Flight in all its glory at Coningsby.

Right on cue. PZ865/Q slips into position perfectly beside the camera ship.

"anti-climactic", held no nasty surprises, thanks to the Hurricane experience. It is skittish in terms of ground-handling thanks to the narrow-track undercarriage, heats up rapidly due to the undercarriage of the early marks blanking the radiators, and will generally run away with you on tarmac at anything much above idle rpm when compared with a Hurri; rather like an F-4 with or without external fuel tanks. It could be generally stated that your problems in a Spit are over once the take-off run commences – until the moment of truth of the landing. That statement assumes a conservative application of power,

though it is possible to raise the tail from a standing start, given a sufficiently strong set of leg muscles.

'The "change-hands" exercise to raise the gear after take-off presents a pilot-induced oscillation problem for the unwary, particularly if combined with a loose throttle friction setting (perhaps the origin of the "one-armed paper-hanger" quotation?) These factors out of the way, the actual flying is pure magic, and even proved to be so on my first solo. Up until then I had believed the Hunter to be the yardstick for "flyable" aeroplanes, but I rapidly changed my mind. The balance and response to controls I found astonishing. More demanding

than the Hurri in terms of countering power and "G" with rudder, but so responsive as to be capable of 3G at the behest of one finger, and a roll rate almost up among some of the fairly agile jet fighters. Add a well-mannered stall either clean or dirty, aerodynamics which allow the Merlin to produce real acceleration against the Hurricane's slow response, and a reasonable view from the bubble canopy though the large elliptical wing and extensive nose, and it would no doubt horrify F-16 drivers in terms of what you can't see.

'Landing the Spit is another matter, which should be simple.

Sqn Ldr 'Shiney' Simmons shows how it's done in XIX PS915. ('Sid' Siddell)

Given a modern runway there is no validity in the constantly curved approach theory, but I suppose it looks good (except from a XIX). The real problem is the very responsive elevator combined with what you think is the right height for touchdown based on the view from the Hurri, where the pilot sits much higher. This produced a wonderful descending stair-step as a result of the change-hands exercise on take-off. Additionally, it would be apparent to most aviators that a light, large-area fin combined with the narrow-track landing gear makes the Spit a bit of a handful in a crosswind. And so it is. Three and a half years on I can now make a fair attempt at a three-pointer in the right place, but I remember my first fifty or so landings as being a new and exciting experience every time.

'Six weeks later, in June 1982, I checked out in the Griffon-engined Spitfire XIX, thus completing the BBMF collection of a Mk IIA, Mk VB and the two Mk XIXs. The XIX appeals to the brute force and ignorance concept bred into me by the F-4, and indeed I enjoy it a good deal. As a straight-line, high-speed machine it is hard to beat as big pistons go, but loses out over the Merlin Spits in noticeably reduced agility due to the higher

Above: *Evocative evening view of PS915 airborne from Norwich.*

Below: *Wg Cdr Dave 'Harrow' Harrison, OC Ops, in Spitfire IIA P7350 over Norfolk.*

ABOVE: *PA474, flown by Sqn Ldr Dave Thomas, and Spitfire XIX PS915, flown by Sqn Ldr 'Shiney' Simmons, near Norwich on Battle of Britain Day, 13 September 1999. PA474 joined the Flight at Coltishall in November 1973.*

LEFT: *XIX PS915, flown by Grp Capt Peter Ruddock, and XIX PM631, piloted by Sqn Ldr Clive Rowley.*

FACING PAGE: *Grp Capt Peter Ruddock in PM631 peels away over Lincolnshire.*

ABOVE: *XIX PM631, flown by Grp Capt Peter Ruddock, over the Fens.*

FACING PAGE: *Tribute. Wg Cdr Dave 'Harrow' Harrison, OC Ops, in P7350 passing Swanton Morley, the famous Norfolk light bomber airfield, which was hosting a reunion for former Arnold Scheme veterans and the Spitfire Society.*

wing-loading. Despite its impressive power output, the Griffon 66 is very sensitive to throttle mishandling, as witnessed by more than one embarrassed pilot who has come to a silent stop on the taxiway due to excessive demands at the low end of the range. The curved windscreen is an aerodynamic wonder – and a visual nightmare. The middle three inches give a reasonable perspective on the outside world; not so the bits at the side through which one peers during most of the classic curved approach, only to roll out much closer to Mother Earth than was previously apparent.

'I feel the best plaudit I can offer Mitchell's masterpiece is this. No matter what air display, no matter what super-agile, mega-powered heavy metal is present, no matter how their pilots speak with pride and affection of their mounts, at the end of the day they will, to a man, cast a wistful glance at the Spitfire and declaim, "I'd give anything to fly that!"'

THE BOSTON BASH

Amazing as it sounds, there are people who believe that air-to-air shoots are carried out at the drop of a hat, or as soon as the sun appears from behind the cloud! Someone has even remarked how lucky it was that this Spitfire passed by our Yak camera ship as we flew over Lincolnshire! Nothing, of course, could be further from the truth. This is because of air traffic rules. Putting together an air-to-air session is an exact science, involving (as far as the BBMF are concerned, anyway) a face-to-face briefing with all aircrews and photographer before take-off, and only after all essential considerations have been agreed upon. It is no good turning up at Coningsby in a Cessna 172 with a pilot who is not formation-qualified and hoping to fly with the BBMF. (Importantly, a recent prerequisite imposed raised the top speed required of the camera ship by 15 knots, from 135 knots to 150 knots.)

Each time the make-up of a shoot changes a new brief must take place. Ideally, it is preferable to brief at the take-off location, but if this is not possible then it involves having to travel before the actual day to Coningsby for the face-to-face, by road or air, or both. Every landing by the camera ship attracts a fee, and if you have to land before the next air-to-air of the day (as in the case of the 'three-in-one' – see chapter – Sorties, the fees and fuel increase accordingly!)

Of course, all these preparations are for naught if weather or unserviceability, or both, prevent the shoot taking place at all. The frustration was never more heartfelt than when Dale and I tried five times without success to do an air-to-air with the Lancaster.

On the debut shoot for this book, on Monday, 31 August 1997, an English public holiday synonymous with bad weather, the gods really made amends for the recent bout of foul conditions. The wallpaper-paste skies parted over Lincolnshire and it

First of the 'firsts'. IIA P7350, flown by Group Captain Al Lockwood, RAF Coningsby station commander, and LFIXE MK356, flown by Sqn Ldr Paul Day, on the occasion of the public debut of these two Spitfires.

First break. Grp Capt Al Lockwood peels away.

was a case of 'nothing but blue skies from now on' instead of hoping 'grey skies are gonna clear up!' Everyone put on a happy face too (and wobbly legs with butterflies in the stomach for good measure on the part of the photographer) when the identity of the two BBMF Spitfires for the planned air-to-air shoot *en route* to the Aylsham Show, Norfolk, was made known. They were IIA P7350, the oldest airworthy Spitfire in the world, and LFIXE MK356. The exciting news was that it was MK356's first display flight following full restoration at St Athan, which meant that it had never been photographed air-to-air before in public. (Apart from an air test carried out by the 'Major' in November 1997, MK356 had not flown since June 1944, some fifty-three years earlier.) What a debut performance for the first BBMF air-to-air session by the

photographer!

Dale piloted the Yak-52 camera ship while the pilots for the 'scoop shoot' were Sqn Ldr Paul Day AFC, flying MK356, and Grp Capt Al Lockwood, RAF Coningsby station commander, flying P7350.

For this first shoot with the BBMF I decided to KISS – 'keep it simple, stupid'. The two Spitfires would formate off our port side, with MK356 nearest, and then a swap would place P7350 nearest the camera. Fortunately, Paul Day suggested that they perform two break sequences. The first break gave me an ideal opportunity to change to 50 ASA Velvia from Fuji Sensia 100 ASA (which I had loaded five minutes prior to take-off after waiting in vain for the sun to appear; it finally did a minute after we took off!)

The shoot offered an opportunity to feature Boston, and in particular its

272-foot-high St Botolph's church tower, as an interesting backdrop. My concentration must have been such that although I took two portrait shots of the two Spitfires passing the 'Stump', as it is popularly known, I could not recall doing so – and these were the only two portrait shots I took on the entire shoot; the other seventy-plus were all landscape shots! Subconsciously, perhaps, I must have switched the camera to the upright at the point we passed the 'Stump'. It was certainly a ghost of a chance.

The icing on the cake was that the Mayor of Boston received a framed print of the two Spitfires over the 'Stump'. It must have brought him great delight, because during the war he flew Spitfires.

With the shoot in the bag, surely it would be 'blue skies' all the way from now on? Nothing could have been further from the truth.

ABOVE: *P7350 and MK356 passing Fosdyke on the River Welland, Lincolnshire, near The Wash.*

BELOW: *Ringing the changes. P7350 now takes centre stage, with MK356 off to port.*

Final break. Sqn Ldr Paul Day peels away and will rejoin P7350 for the onward flight to Aylsham, Norfolk, while the Yak-52 camera ship team heads for Fenland airfield near Holbeach St Johns and lunch.

SORTIES

Press on regardless – never mind the weather
Press on regardless – it's a piece of cake
Press on regardless – we'll all press on together
Cos you're bound to see the Dummer or the Steinhuder Lake.
– To the tune of 'Poor Joey'

Wind beneath my wings. P7350, south of Marham, is a tribute to the Canon's image stabiliser, which, despite severe buffeting in the open cockpit of the Yak-52, does well to stay sharp. Image is everything!

Our second sortie with the BBMF, on 20 September, was similar to the 'Boston Bash' in that it looked like the bad weather on the morning of the shoot would interfere with flying and possibly force a 'scrub'. As we took off in the Yak-52 from the Touch Down Aero Centre at Old Buckenham, Norfolk, that Sunday morning, it seemed that bad weather north of the Wash would prevent Wg Cdr Dave 'Harrow' Harrison in P7350 from making our briefed rendezvous south of King's Lynn. However, Dave skilfully

FACING PAGE: LFIXE MK356 and IIA P7350 passing Boston's 272-foot-high St Botolph's church tower, or the 'Stump' as it is popularly known, which dominates the flat fenland countryside for miles around (RAF Coningsby was granted the Freedom of the Borough on 16 May 1963). Once a beacon for coastal navigators on The Wash, the 'Stump' was used as a recognition point by the Luftwaffe. From the top, on a clear day, it is possible to see Lincoln Cathedral nearly thirty miles away.

Regal lady. Wg Cdr Harrison pulls P7350 in tight on the camera ship for a classic pose.

'rollercoasted' over the low stratus covering the Wash and a very pleasant flight to Norwich Airport via Swanton Morley open day ensued – albeit with the Yak's rear cockpit hood fully back and gale-force winds buffeting the two cameras. (There's nothing worse than a loose Canon.) Results once again were excellent, but from now on the weather was to dog our every effort.

FAMOUS FIVE

We were recommended by Paul Day to keep 22 September clear, but not informed why; a nod from the 'Major' that something special was to occur was good enough for me. On the day in question Dale and Dave Puleston, remarkably, scraped in on VFR limits and positioned the Yak at Coningsby while the massed ranks of the press gathered expectantly with a C-130 Hercules of 70 Squadron in attendance. Once airborne, they were to photograph from the ramp of the Herc not one, not two, not even three, but all five BBMF Spitfires! All five have not flown in formation before or since. Dale and I would sortie alone in the Yak-52 and hopefully photograph them off our port side.

Unfortunately, a Lincolnshire fog any Hollywood special effects man would have been proud of had descended over Coningsby and a layer of thick cloud prevented the sun from burning it off, so it cloaked proceedings for most of the day. The eleven o'clock briefing to the assembled throng took place, but take-off time came and went, and went again, and again. A lull followed in the afternoon while HRH Princess Margaret visited the station, then finally, at five o'clock, up went the C-130, the Yak, and a score of disgruntled photographers.

On days such as this Cynicism with a capital 'C' is part of the photographer's outlook (on the basis that if everything comes together it's an unexpected bonus). Everyone was convinced they would get nothing to speak of on film. Ninety-nine per cent of them didn't (due mainly to the weather but also because video cameramen on board the C-130 insisted on using long-range fixed lenses). The Yak-52 pilot, and the photographer nestling in the rear seat, literally scooped all five Spitfires flying off the port side in echelon high.

Teeing up the shot. Wg Cdr Harrison switches sides over the Wensum Valley golf club on the eastern approaches to Norwich.

THE SHOOT THAT NEVER WAS

How is the Met, sir, how is the Met, sir,
How is the Met? – It looks very dud to me.
Let's scrub it out, sir, let's scrub it out, sir,
'Cos I've got a date fixed with my popsie.

Attention now turned to the prize I had been seeking ever since the BBMF left Coltishall near my home in Norwich, in early 1976. If the five-Spitfire formation was the summit, then the Lancaster was, for me, the pinnacle. On 27 September Dale, Dave and I drove to Coningsby for the briefing. The Lanc was to fly to Flixton, Suffolk, and we were to do the air-to-air from the Yak-52 again. The weather had other ideas. This was particularly galling for us, but especially so for the Lanc pilot, Sqn Ldr Dave Buchanan. Dave wanted a memorable shoot as this was his last week on RAF flying duty (flying AWACs at Waddington) before a posting to a desk job in Scotland.

It was not to be. Rain pelted down and it was decided to postpone, especially as there was the chance of a longer air-to-air session on the Wednesday or Thursday when training flights only were scheduled, but twice that week the sessions were

Get on parade! All the Spitfires get ready for the off for the first ever appearance of all five Memorial Flight Spitfires in a single formation on 22 September 1998. (Dave Puleston)

'scrubbed' because of continual bad weather. Ironically, on the Friday, when the Lanc was due at the twenty-fifth anniversary of the Jaguar celebrations at RAF Coltishall, blue skies appeared, but Dave could not get a crew together! Only one chance remained: the Saturday. As a Spitfire would now accompany the Lanc it meant that we would have to drive to Coningsby for a new briefing.

Saturday morning was again filled with black clouds and heavy rain, but at briefing spirits were lifted. I said ideally I would like to photograph the Lanc and Spitfire V near Norwich Cathedral (Paul Day had arranged for AB910 to fly instead

of the II or IX, which we had photographed twice before). Also, Al Lockwood ceremoniously 'binned' the original route, where we would have joined north of the city and flown to King's Lynn, and introduced a new one. The pair would now fly straight across Norwich! Elated, I asked Dave Buchanan if he could, after Norwich, fly with the bomb-bay doors open. He smiled and said that it would be no problem, and would I like him to put on thirty degrees of bank as well? The two pilots also worked out a plan so that I could photograph them singularly and together . . . bliss!

Our return to Old Buckenham

though, was in vain. It ended in utter desolation as the weather quite clearly prevented us from even thinking about getting the Yak out of its hangar. Our fifth and final attempt had failed. It would be a year before we 'got' the Lanc.

AIR FORCE BLUE STILL GOING STRONG

We are the heavy bombers, we try to do our bit,
We fly through concentrations of flak with sky all lit.

July 1999 was a wonderful month for blue skies, promising a memorable Saturday the 31st. Predictions were

Take five. The C-130K has gone and it's our turn. In this, the first ever appearance of all five Memorial Flight Spitfires, are: LFIXE MK356, flown by Sqn Ldr Paul Day; IIA P7350, flown by Grp Capt Al Lockwood, Coningsby station commander; VB AB910, piloted by Sqn Ldr 'Shiney' Simmons; XIX PS915, flown by Wg Cdr Dave Harrison, OC Ops; and XIX PM631, flown by Sqn Ldr Clive Rowley.

that the BBMF would offer us three shoots in one day: first on the menu was the Dakota and two Spitfires, which were scheduled to display in Belgium; second session would be the much sought after Lancaster, which would be on its way to do flypasts at Waddington and Bardney, then to Southampton for an overnight stopover before doing a show on the Sunday; thirdly, another Spitfire, also on a solo flight, would carry out a flyby at Huntingdon.

Unfortunately, at Fairford on 25 July P7350 lost engine power at 100 feet during a flypast and Wg Cdr Nick Watson, who was on his first season with the Flight, chandelled up to gain height and to place the fighter into wind before using the emergency gear-lowering system and landing on the main runway without engine power. P7350 seemed to have a serious crankcase failure. This problem could manifest itself in the other Merlins used by the BBMF, so that week all the Merlin-engined

Busted flush. Grp Capt Al Lockwood (left) confers with Sqn Ldr Dave Buchanan (right). Sgt Andy Bishop, the Lanc air engineer, looks on. A New Zealander who joined the RAF in the early 1970s, Al Lockwood began a tour flying the C-130 Hercules, later flying fighters in 1977, firstly on the Phantom on 43(F) Squadron, then as one of the initial cadre of instructors for the Tornado GR.1. He converted to the Tornado F.3 and completed flying tours on 5 and 29(F) Squadrons as well as ground tours at Ramstein, Germany, and with BAe Warton. With over 5,500 hours of flying, he took command of RAF Coningsby on 12 December 1996. Al was on his second season with the Flight. Dave joined the RAF in 1965 and flew Shackleton, Nimrod and AWACS aircraft, amassing 11,000 flying hours. It was Dave's third and final season with the BBMF, and this was his last week as a QFI on 23 Squadron's Sentry aircraft at Waddington, before moving to a desk job. Despite their best efforts at briefing, the shoot could not be shot.

fighters were grounded. (This exacerbated the shortage of Merlins, which had developed earlier in the season to the extent that the Lanc needed three replacement Merlins and these had to be obtained from the Spitfires and Hurricanes.)

Also, there was a last-minute doubt about the Dakota for the 31st; if it was not capable of flying, it would mean that the Spitfires would not go to Belgium either. This state of affairs would leave just the two Griffon-engined Spitfire XIXs and the Lanc.

On Monday it looked like all three shoots were finished. Then the first two were still on, although the Dakota was in for maintenance for the next two days and would miss the Lowestoft two-day show. I tried to be philosophical about the situation as I had already 'got' all five Spitfires in one fell swoop. I desperately wanted the Lanc, however, having tried and failed on five previous occasions.

By Friday we had been overtaken

Arnhem recalled. Grp Capt Peter Ruddock, Coningsby station commander, in PM631, with Dakota ZA947 flown by Sqn Ldr Dave Thomas.

by events which ruled out the third session and pared down the first to one Spitfire XIX (because there was a problem with the propeller on the other XIX) plus the Dakota. Thankfully, the Lanc air-to-air was still on. Actually, losing the third shoot was a blessing in disguise because it made the day much simpler to plan. Not having to land again after shooting the Lanc meant we could have longer alongside the bomber, and we would not have to return to Coningsby, with the consequent saving of fuel and a third landing fee. Even so, the day would

still be busy. Pilots have to work out how, when and where to be times three, or, now, times two. Fuel, weight, air time, etc., all have to be taken into consideration. All I had to worry about, meanwhile, was the number of films to use on each shoot.

The day would start with a landing at Coningsby an hour before the first face-to-face briefing, then the shoot with the Dakota (piloted by Sqn Ldr Dave Thomas) and XIX PM631 (piloted by Grp Capt Peter Ruddock) would take place. This would be followed by a second landing and the second face-to-face briefing an hour

before the Lancaster (piloted by Flt Lt Giles 'Grubsy' Smerdon) shoot.

Personally, if I could only 'get' the Lanc I knew I would be more than happy, especially if we could get it passing Lincoln Cathedral. At the end of the day, it would be down to the most important governing factor: weather!

As things turned out the weather was glorious – if anything it was too hazy – and although I could not persuade 'Grubsy' to let us do Lincoln Cathedral (he had to 'throw some boxes out' at Waddington and Bardney, and time was therefore

On the Boston Beat. Grp Capt Peter Ruddock overflies the town.

against us) everything went well. At briefing Peter Ruddock agreed to fly PM631 along the coastline. The shoot over Lincolnshire, and the blue against blue sea, was something to behold. We landed, briefed again, and took off to rendezvous with the Lanc over Sleaford, before heading south-south-east over Lincolnshire, Leicestershire and Northamptonshire. I was captivated by the Lanc's majesty and power.

Shortly after passing RAF Cottesmore, Dale spotted the Eye Brook Reservoir near Uppingham, Rutland (see page 97) he led us and the Lanc (bomb-bay doors open) right across it, Dambusters-style! At briefing, 'Grubsy' had graciously agreed to do a 'Dave Buchanan', and sure enough he opened the bomb-bay doors, peeling away with them still open, as agreed, for a magnificent finale!

SPIT AND POLISH

We had now accomplished every shoot possible, apart from the two elusive Hurricanes and AB910, which, it will be remembered, were grounded through lack of available engines. An opportunity now arose whereby we could photograph the Lanc and a Spitfire XIX transiting from Southend Airport during the two-day Clacton Air Show (26 to 27 August). The first dilemma was: which day? Whatever I chose, it would be Sod's law the other day would have better weather. I went for the second day, mainly so we could photograph the pair returning to Coningsby after the show. This would permit more time than if we photographed them in transit. As it turned out, the weather was very good, and the results were fantastic.

We briefed in the terminal at Southend Airport with Grp Capt Peter Ruddock, pilot of PM631 again, and Sqn Ldr Dave Thomas, the Lanc pilot. Because the nose art is on the left of both aircraft Peter would close in on our starboard side, with the

ABOVE: *If it's Tuesday, it must be Belgium. Grp Capt Peter Ruddock and Dave Thomas* en route *for the Continent.*

BELOW: *Shades of blue.*

ABOVE: *It Ain't Half Hot, Mum.*
Probably the first ever air-to-air photo
of the BBMF Lanc flying with bomb-bay
doors open. Not only are the bomb-bay
doors open, so are the two upper
fuselage hatches.

RIGHT: *Flt Lt Giles Smerdon. 'Grubsy'*
joined the RAF in 1983. He flew
Canberras before converting to the
Tornado F.3 and then served with 23
and 25 Squadrons before joining 56(R)
Squadron, the Tornado OCU, as a
tactics instructor. This was his third
and final season with the BBMF, but his
first full 'tour' as a Lancaster captain,
having completed his conversion at the
end of the 1998 season.

ABOVE: *Reining her in. 'Grubsy' does a magnificent job given the hot and sometimes turbulent conditions, working hard on the controls of* City of Lincoln *as it tries to become a bucking bronco.*

RIGHT: *Enemy coast ahead? J-Johnnie's front office hoves beautifully into view.*

ABOVE: *Still going strong. PA474 high over Cottesmore.*

BELOW: *Keeping up. No 'Upkeep' bomb but Flt Lt Smerdon re-enacts the Dambusters raid especially for us over Rutland Water.*

Bombs gone!

ABOVE: *Leader's benefit in tight formation. PA474, flown by Sqn Ldr Dave Thomas, and Spitfire XIX PS915, flown by Grp Capt Peter Ruddock,* en route *from Southend to Coningsby via Ely, Cambridgeshire.*

LEFT: *All roads lead to Ely.*

FACING PAGE: *PA474 and PS915 over historic Ely Cathedral. In the north choir aisle of the cathedral is a memorial stained-glass window to 2, 3, 8 and 100 Groups RAF, all of which flew from airfields in the surrounding countryside during World War Two.*

Lanc then joining slightly behind. Dave Thomas, who had been in the background flying the Dak on the July shoot, asked, tongue-in-cheek (at least I think it was tongue-in-cheek), 'Are we going to get in on the shoot this time?' As we had captured the Lanc in all its glory on the July shoot I wanted to put the Lanc far out with the Spitfire nearest. Peter would stay closest to the camera ship throughout, while the Lanc would be the backdrop. I requested that each time Peter moved the Spitfire up, could Dave go low, and every time the Spit went low, could the Lanc fly higher? Effectively, the Lanc filled the 'hole' behind the Spit. I also pushed my luck and asked Dave if he could bank and dip his wing slightly to add to the overall effect. He graciously agreed!

As the briefing closed, an unexpected bonus for a 'grand finale' opened up, one which I seized upon immediately. As we would be flying near Mildenhall and Lakenheath, it was mooted that for obvious reasons it might be wise to give the bases a wider berth. This meant we would fly further to the west, near Ely. I immediately threw my hat into the ring and asked if we could overfly the famous cathedral in close formation. It was agreed, and we did. The results are obvious for all to see.

As a footnote, I employed the same tactics for the evening shoot over Norfolk (see chapter Their Finest Hour), where Dave Thomas, aware of the wider picture, stayed in the background once more while 'Shiney' Simmons this time 'hogged' the centre stage superbly.

ABOVE: *Our Prayers answered. Sunday 7th May 2000 and the opportunity was taken to become the very first to photograph PA474 air-to-air in its splendid new* Mickey The Moocher *livery, over Lincolnshire, and along the coast near Skegness. The crew for this momentous occasion was Flt Lt Merv Counter and Sqn Ldr Stu Reid (pilots), Sqn Ldr Andy Marson (navigator) and Flight Sgt Phil McConville (air engineer).*

FACING PAGE: *Heading home. PA474 peels away as PS915 continues over Cambridgeshire, but not before the radio waves hum with anticipation of a potentially unique shoot.*

SONG OF THE MERLIN

Touch me gently, wake me softly,
Let me start to sing,
Free to use my strength and power
Throbbing on the wing.

Let me sing of men returning
Safely homeward bound,
Then my thrusting heart shall sing
In glorious joyful sound.
– from 'The Song of the Merlin' by Audrey Grealy

HURRICANE IIC LF363

LF363 was built at Langley, Buckinghamshire, and first flew on 1 January 1944. On 28 January the Hurricane was delivered to 5 MU at RAF Kemble, Gloucestershire. Believed to be the last Hurricane to enter service, LF363 was issued to 63 Squadron at Turnhouse, Midlothian, on 30 March 1944, moving two months later to 309 (Polish) Squadron at Drem, East Lothian. LF363 completed at least eighteen operational sorties with the Poles before going to 22 MU, Silloth, Cumberland, on 1 November 1944. On 30 November it was allocated to 26 Squadron. Unlike many other Hurricanes, LF363 was not scrapped at the end of the war. In July 1957 LF363 became a founder member of the RAF Historic Flight at Biggin Hill. In 1968 it appeared with the rest of the fighters of the BBMF in the film epic *The Battle of Britain*.

On 11 September 1991, while *en route* from Coningsby to Jersey, the aircraft's engine started running rough, pouring smoke from all twelve exhaust stubs. The pilot, Sqn Ldr Allan 'Slam' Martin, attempted to land at Wittering, but the engine then failed completely, resulting in a crash-landing on the airfield. Martin suffered some burns and a broken ankle as he scrambled away from the fierce fire which engulfed the

Last of the Many. Mk IIC PZ865 was the 14,533rd and final Hurricane built, so it is appropriate that it is operated by the BBMF.

Second to None. Hurricane Mk IIC LF363, flown by Grp Capt Peter Ruddock, looks as good as the day it was built. As everyone now knows – Hurris shot down more enemy aircraft in the Battle of Britain than the more famous Spitfire.

Hurricane. LF363 rejoined the Flight in September 1998 after a total rebuild and was painted US-C of 56 Squadron.

HURRICANE IIC PZ865

PZ865 was the last Hurricane of 14,533 to be built. During construction at Langley, Buckinghamshire, a banner, 'Last of the Many', hung over the assembly line and this inscription was transferred to PZ865's port side when it rolled off the production line in 1944. PZ865 never saw service with the RAF, being used by Hawker mainly as a communications and test aircraft. Registered G-AMAU, the Hurricane took part in several air races, finishing second in the 1950 King's Cup Air Race sponsored by HRH the Princess Margaret (honorary commandant, RAF Coningsby).

During the early 1960s, PZ865 was employed as a chase plane on development flights involving the P1127 'Kestrel'. In late 1971 PZ865 was given a complete overhaul and in March 1972 flown to RAF Coltishall and given to the Flight by Hawker. She was flown back to RAF Coningsby on 4 March 1999 after a major overhaul by chief technician Andy Benn and his team of three full-time engineers at RAF St Athan. New

Spitfire VB AB910 at IWM Duxford. In 1997, when AB910 was dismantled and airfreighted across the Atlantic, carrying the markings of 71 (Eagle) Squadron, for the USAF celebrations in America, the aircraft was painted in the markings of ZD-C of 222 (Natal) Squadron.

top panels on the wing roots were made and fitted, inboard leading-edge skins replaced, and a complete engine cowling constructed. All of the fighter's control surfaces and rear fuselage were given a total refabric. After successful engine tests PZ865 was repainted in the colours of 5 Squadron, coded 'Q', of Air Command SE Asia.

SPITFIRE IIA P7350

Ordered on 12 April 1938, P7350 is the fourteenth of 11,939 Spitfires built at the Castle Bromwich 'Shadow Factory', Birmingham. In all, 920 IIs were built, 750 of them completed as IIAs with eight machine guns (the 170 IIBs had four 0.303in guns and two 20mm cannon). Test flown in August 1940, P7350 was issued to 266 (Rhodesia) Squadron at RAF Wittering on 6 September and was coded 'UO-T'. On 17 October 1940 P7350 was one of fourteen IIs transferred to 603 (City of Edinburgh) Squadron, AAF. On or about 25 October, P7350 saw combat with Bf 109s and was forced to crash-land. The repaired bullet holes can still be seen. During the war, P7350 suffered three Cat. B flying accidents while serving with various units, including 616 (County of South Yorkshire) Squadron, AAF, at Tangmere, 64

Squadron at Hornchurch, and finally the Central Gunnery School at RAF Sutton Bridge near King's Lynn, before being put into storage at Colerne on 24 July 1944.

Since joining the Flight in October 1968 P7350 has worn many codes. During its winter overhaul 1996–7, P7350 was painted to represent P8509 BA-Y *The Old Lady* (given to the RAF by the Bank of England, affectionately known as the 'Old Lady of Threadneedle Street') of 277 Search and Rescue Squadron operating from RAF Hawkinge in Kent. A shortage of a Merlin engine meant that the aircraft was not flown at displays until September. P7350

Oh to be in England now that summer's here! Spitfire IIA P7350 piloted by Wg Cdr Dave Harrison.

Since the end of the 1998 season LF363 appeared (briefly, because of the shortage of Merlin engines) as R4197 US-C of 56 (Punjab) Squadron, representing a Hurricane based at North Weald in 1940. (Significantly, 56 Squadron's crest is a phoenix rising from the ashes.)

appeared in the colours of 277 Squadron ASR for just two seasons, 1997–8, before changing in spring 1999 to XT-D L1067 *Blue Peter*, a Mk I airframe, of 603 (City of Edinburgh) Squadron, to mark the seventy-fifth anniversary of the Auxiliary Air Force.

Blue Peter, which was named after a famous racehorse of the period, was flown by the CO of 603, Sqn Ldr (later Grp Capt) George Lovell Denholm. 'Uncle George', as he was affectionately known, was born at Bo'Ness, West Lothian, Scotland, on 20 December 1908, and he joined the AAF in 1933, serving

with 603 for six years until the unit was mobilised in August 1939, by which time he had become a flight commander. On 16 October 1939 Flt Lt Denholm was involved in the action that brought down the first enemy aircraft over Britain when twelve Heinkel He 111s attacked cruisers in the Firth of Forth. He was awarded a half share of a He 111, one of two shot down by 602 and 603 Squadrons, and the first German aircraft brought down over Britain since 1918.

On 17 March 1940 Denholm, flying L1067, damaged a Do 17 two miles east of Aberdeen. On 4 June

1940 he took command of 603 Squadron and on 26 June he claimed a He 111. On 3 July, leading Red Section, he was awarded a third share in the destruction of a Ju 88 of 8/KG 30, forty miles east of Peterhead. On 28 August, with his squadron now based at Hornchurch, Denholm was awarded a probable Bf 109E west of Canterbury, and a confirmed Bf 109E ten miles west of Manston. On 30 August, flying L1067 *Blue Peter* again, he was shot down over Deal, Kent, by Bf 110s, and he bailed out safely before the fighter crashed at Hope Farm, Snargate.

Further engagements with enemy

aircraft continued during September with claims of aircraft destroyed, probable or damaged, including another descent by parachute on 15 September. Denholm was awarded the DFC on 22 October 1940. He finished the war with a total of three victories and three shared destroyed, one unconfirmed destroyed, three and one shared probables, and six damaged. Grp Capt Denholm DFC left the RAF in 1947, having been station commander at North Weald. He died in June 1997 aged eighty-eight.

SPITFIRE VB AB910

Originally ordered as a Mk I on 22 June 1940, AB910 came off the production line at Castle Bromwich in 1941 as a VB and was issued to 222 (Natal) Squadron at North Weald on 22 August. AB910 later served with 130 (Punjab) Squadron and 133 (Eagle) Squadron. In August 1942, 133 Squadron was operating from Lympne. On 19 August, when the Eagle Squadron was ordered to patrol the Dieppe area on Operation *Jubilee*, AB910 flew four sorties, three of them by Flg Off Doorly. On his second patrol in AB910 he shared in the destruction of two Fw 190s and a Ju 88, while four more Fw 190s and three Do 217s were damaged. Earlier that day, flying BL773, Flt Sgt (later

All in a day's work. Cannon armed PZ865/Q (in the markings of 5 Squadron) and LF363 US-C (in the markings of 56 Squadron) returning to Coningsby from Old Warden following their display, and an earlier rendezvous with two Tornado F.3s (also from 5 and 56 Squadrons) for a photo-shoot en route for the BBMF.

AB910 is brought out of the hangar at Coningsby for the abortive air-to-air shoot. While the other Spitfires have changed their colours almost as many times in a season as Manchester Utd, AB910 has worn the same livery for several years.

1st Lt) Richard L. 'Dixie' Alexander shot down a Fw 190. On his third patrol, flying AB910, the American from Grant Park, Illinois, shot down a Do 217 south of Dieppe.

On 2 September 1942 AB910 was transferred to 242 'Canadian' Squadron and it later served with 416 'City of Oshawa' and 402 'Winnipeg Bear' Squadrons RCAF. While at 53 OTU Hibaldstow, on 9 February

1945, AB910 took off with ACW2 Margaret Horton, who had no time to dismount and was still on the tail. Flt Lt Neil Cox, the pilot, made one circuit and, with the aircraft handling strangely, landed, still with a very frightened WAAF wrapped around the tail!

AB910 was finally 'demobbed' in June 1947 and was used for air racing. In 1953, after a heavy landing

during the King's Cup Air Race, AB910 was returned to Vickers Armstrong, rebuilt, and later operated in its original livery. Vickers presented AB910 to the RAF, and on 16 September 1965 it was flown to Coltishall by Jeffrey Quill, the company's chief test pilot. During 1968 AB910 took part in the film *The Battle of Britain*. On 20 August 1978 it was involved in a taxiing accident

Wg Cdr Dave Harrison dons his bone dome prior to his BoB Day display over Norwich.

Sqn Ldr Clive Rowley checks everything's OK at the back. Clive joined the RAF in 1970 and, following pilot training, flew Lightnings on 19 Squadron at RAF Gütesloh, Germany. Subsequently, he became a QFI and completed tours on the Bulldog and on the Hawk at 2 TWU. He then returned to flying 'Frightenings' at RAF Binbrook, where he served on 11 and 5 Squadrons and as OC the LTF. In 1987 he was posted to RAF Coningsby to fly the Tornado F.3, initially as a Flt Cdr on 5 Squadron, then as a trials pilot with the F.3 OEU. With over 6,000 hours of flying Clive is now a specialist aircrew instructor with 56(R) Squadron. The year 2000 is his fifth season with the BBMF.

during an airshow at Bex in Switzerland. It was recovered to Abingdon for a major rebuild and then to Kemble for full servicing. AB910 did not fly again until 27 October 1981, when it rejoined the Flight.

Early in 1997 AB910 was dismantled and airfreighted across the Atlantic, carrying the markings of 71 (Eagle) Squadron, for the USAF celebrations in America before returning to the UK and the planned

repainting of the aircraft in 222 (Natal) Squadron colours as ZD-C, which the aircraft carried for the 1999 season.

SPITFIRE LF.IXC MK356

MK356 was built at Castle Bromwich early in 1944 and was issued to 443 (Hornet) Squadron RCAF at RAF Digby, Lincolnshire, on 11 March. A

week later a move was made to Holmsley South, Hampshire, to form 144 Canadian Wing (commanded by Wg Cdr 'Johnny' Johnson), 2nd TAF, to prepare for the imminent invasion of France.

Flg Off (later General) Gordon F. Ockenden, an 'old twenty-year-old' from Vermilion, Alberta, flew MK356 for the first time on 18 March. After Armament Practice Camp at Hutton Cranswick between 27 March and 7 April, 443 Squadron moved to

PZ865 was repainted in the colours of 5 Squadron, coded 'Q', of Air Command SE Asia. 5 Squadron, which had been an Army Co-operation unit in India in 1941, fully re-equipped with Hurricane IICs in mid-1943 and returned to action in December 1943, undertaking a variety of bomber escort and strafing duties until June 1944, when it again withdrew to India, and converted to P-47 Thunderbolts. After major servicing by Rolls-Royce at Filton during winter 1992–3, PZ865 was returned to the BBMF following a complete refabric and repaint in the desert camouflage colours of Hurricane I P3731/J of 261 Squadron, one of twelve aircraft flown off HMS Argus in Operation Hurry, the relief of Malta, in September 1940.

Westhampnett (8 April) flying their first op on the 13th, when they provided top-cover escort for Bostons and Mitchells bombing Dieppe. On 14 April 'Gord' Ockenden flew MK356 on its first 'op' (he flew it on nineteen altogether), a one-hour-fifty-minute Rodeo, Compiègne–Paris–Rouen, encountering light flak. On 22 April Hornet Squadron moved to Funtingdon, Sussex, and by 15 May was at Ford on the Sussex coast.

On D-Day + 1, 7 June, 'Gord' flew two patrols, Bayeux to Caen. On the second patrol, in MK356, four Bf 109Gs were attacked 'on the deck'. Gord chased one of the Messerschmitts and got strikes. Flt Lt Hugh Russell finished him off, the 109 exploded, and each pilot (Russell was KIA, 16 June) was credited with a half share. (Ockenden flew 139 ops and his wartime score reached four confirmed victories, one shared destroyed, and one damaged.)

MK356 probably suffered two belly landings prior to the one that ended its flying career, and was damaged by enemy action on three occasions. On 14 June, MK356 took off from Ford with Flg Off T. G. Monroe at the controls when a wheel came off during take-off. Monroe elected to continue with the operation over France. On the return to Ford, a belly landing was made and as Hornet Squadron moved to a forward base in France, MK356 was put into storage in England.

Post-war, MK356 was used as an instructional airframe, and as a gate guardian, until 1967, when it was used as a ground static airframe in *The Battle of Britain*. After filming, the Spitfire was put on display in the Museum at St Athan.

During the late 1980s it was decided to return MK356 to flying condition. However, the main spars were found to be badly damaged and

a 'new' set of wings were acquired from XVI SL674. These wings had the clipped tips of an LF (low-flying) variant. Until this time the aircraft was fitted with the 'normal' rounded tipped wings. In January 1992 a team from St Athan, led by chief technician Chris Bunn, began a full restoration including evening work with volunteer personnel, culminating in the aircraft's first flight for fifty-three years on 7 November 1997 when Sqn Ldr Paul Day air-tested it from St Athan. MK356 was delivered to the BBMF at RAF Coningsby on 14 November and painted in its original and only operational markings of 2I-V of 443 'Hornet' Squadron RCAF. In April 1998 the Lancaster 'blew' one of its four Merlins and MK356's powerplant was used as a temporary replacement. On 31 August MK356 flew on the display circuit for the first time.

P7350 in the colours of XT-D L1067 Blue Peter, a Mk I airframe, of 603 (City of Edinburgh) Squadron, AAF, at IWM Duxford.

ABOVE: *Various parts of L1067, including the instrument panel, most of the major controls and components, plus portions of engine cowling bearing traces of the name Blue Peter, were uncovered during an excavation by the Brenzett Aeronautical Museum in September 1973.*

('Sid' Siddell)

RIGHT: *Higher than an eagle. Grp Capt Peter Ruddock in the cockpit of Spitfire VB AB910 which once carried the markings of US 71 (Eagle) Squadron.*

ABOVE: *P7350, alias XT-D, catches the sun's rays during an air-to-air session over Lincolnshire.*
('Sid' Siddell)

RIGHT: *'The Pouting Pussy' on the port side of PS915.*

GRIFFON'S GROWL

Shiney's machine. In recent years PS915 has carried the markings of a XIV commemorating the work and development carried out by test pilots of both the A&AEE at Boscombe Down and Supermarine Aviation.

XIX PM631

PM631 was too late to see operational service during the war, being built in November 1945 and having been delivered to the RAF in 1946. On 6 May 1949 PM631 was issued to 203 Advanced Flying School at Keevil, Wiltshire, and was in use until 13 January 1950. Modified for meteorological work, from 2 July 1951 the aircraft was leased to Short Brothers for the Temperature and Humidity Monitoring (THUM) Flight at Hooton Park, Cheshire, and Woodvale in Lancashire, operated by a division of Short Brothers and Harland and flown by civilian pilots. On 11 July 1957, in formation with P5853 and PS915, PM631 was flown to Biggin Hill to form, along with Hurricane LF363, the Historic Aircraft Flight, which was later developed into the BBMF.

ABOVE: *Two thousand horses straining on the leash. One can almost hear the Griffon's growl.*

BELOW: *Bengal lancer. XIX PS915 spent the winter of 1997 at RAF St Athan on major servicing and reappeared representing a XIV in the markings of 152 (Hyderabad) Squadron of SEAC complete with a black panther motif, otherwise known as the 'Pouting Pussy', on the rear fuselage.*

ABOVE: *Blue is the colour. This close-up of Grp Capt Peter Ruddock flying PM631 clearly shows the name of Wg Cdr Donald B. Pearson DFC AFC, who commanded 681 (PR) Squadron SEAC at Alipur, Mingaladon and Kai Tak, April 1945 to May 1946 (681 Squadron, which disbanded on 1 August 1946, did not sport the standard SEAC stripes). A XIX (PS888 of 81 Squadron) made the RAF's last operational Spitfire sortie, in Malaya on 1 April 1954.*

LEFT: *Achtung Spitfire! 'Shiney' Simmons positions PS915 perfectly for the camera.*

ABOVE: *Grp Capt Peter Ruddock in PM631 skirting The Wash. The XIX was the final unarmed photo-recce version of the Spitfire to be built for the RAF and was something of a hybrid, being basically a XIV airframe with modified VC wings.*

BELOW: *Grp Capt Peter Ruddock 'firing up' (literally).* (Dale Featherby)

The two other XIXs were relegated to gate guardian duties and other units (PS583 was finally sold on 13 February 1995 and the proceeds were used to pay for the rebuild of Hurricane LF363). PM631, however, remained with the Flight and is the BBMF's longest serving aircraft, 2000 its forty-third year of continuous service on display duties.

XIX PS915

This Spitfire was issued to RAF Benson, Oxfordshire, on 26 April 1945 and served with 541 Squadron and 1 Pilot's Pool, before moving to the PR Development Unit to test new cameras for PR work. Assigned on 8 July 1948 to 2 Squadron at Wunsdorf in Germany, PS915 flew strategic reconnaissance sorties before returning to the UK in 1951. In 1954 PS915 joined the THUM Flight at Woodvale. Together with XIXs PS853 and PM631, PS915 was flown to Biggin Hill on 11 July 1957 as one of the Flight's original Spitfires, but was quickly retired to gate guardian duties, which lasted almost thirty years. After being refurbished to airworthiness and modified to take a Griffon 58 engine by BAe Warton Division, PS915 returned to the Flight in 1987.

ABOVE AND NEXT PAGE: *A brace of 19s as PS915 and PM631 formate.*

I'll shoot 'em down sir,
I'll shoot 'em down, sir,
I'll shoot 'em down
if they don't shoot at me.
Then we'll go to the
Ops Room and shoot
a horrid line, sir,
And then we'll all
get the DFC.

ODE TO A DARK LADY

A beauteous comely maid was she,
Her lovely form a joy to see.
She came as swiftly as the night,
As graceful as a bird in flight,
Into the green years of our life,
Not sweetheart true nor loving wife,
But dark, mysterious, proud, unknown,
To cherish, love but never own.
Respectfully we learned to pay,
Our tributes to her day by day,
And as our lives with hers entwined,
Our joys, our fears, our inner mind
Became a mutual living thing
To take upon our journeying.
She opened wide her arms to share
With us the perils of the air;
Her steadfast spirit, loyal, true,
Was with us always as we flew;
She never faltered, even though
She might be wounded, weak and slow.
We raise our glasses, drink a toast,
Remembering a very host
Of things that time cannot transcend,
A gallant mistress, servant, friend,
We loved her to the very end,
My lady Lancaster.

'Ode to a Dark Lady' by Audrey Grealy

City of Lincoln

PA474 was built by Vickers-Armstrong at Chester as a mainstream B.1 reconnaissance/bomber modified for 'Tiger Force' before the Japanese unconditionally surrendered in August 1945. In 1965 PA474 was restored and painted to represent R5508/KM-B, the 44 Squadron aircraft Sqn Ldr John Nettleton flew on the Augsburg raid on 17 April 1942. In 1967, a successful air test was flown and occasional test flights and displays followed. In November 1973 PA474 joined the BBMF at RAF Coltishall. In March 1976 it was moved with the rest of the BBMF to RAF Coningsby. (In 1968, 20,000 Lincolnshire residents had signed a petition, organised by the Lincolnshire Lancaster Appeal Committee, which was sent to the MoD asking if PA474 could be based in their county.)

LEFT: *Merlins racing. Deliveries of the Lancaster began in early 1942 to 44 Squadron at Waddington, followed by 97 Squadron at Woodhall Spa. On 3 March 1942 four aircraft from 44 Squadron flew the first Lancaster operation of the war with a minelaying sortie in the Heligoland Bight. On the night of 10/11 March two Lancasters from 44 Squadron completed the first Lancaster night operation with a raid on Essen.*

BELOW: *'Dambuster' over the Derwent, 19 May 1993. Fifty years earlier the Lancasters of 617 Squadron practised dropping 'bouncing' bombs on water in the Lake District until, on the night of 16/17 May 1943, Operation* Chastise *went ahead and nineteen crews set out to destroy German dams in the Ruhr.*

RIGHT: City of Lincoln *proud and serene. The front turret comes from 1451 Haverhill Squadron ATC, and was exchanged for a dummy Fairey Fireflash missile supplied by the RAF Museum. This organisation also supplied the two .303in machine-guns for the turret.*

(Dale Featherby)

ABOVE: *A different perspective – or should it be 'perspextive'?*

OPPOSITE PAGE: *Trusting. City of Lincoln and 'Major' displaying over Blickling Hall, near Aylsham, Norfolk. During the war Blickling Hall, now owned by the National Trust, was used as an RAF Officer's Mess for airmen from nearby Oulton.*

RIGHT: *Hold the camera in front, point backwards, shoot, and hope you've got both Merlins!*

RIGHT: *À la* Memphis Belle. *PA474 props whip up the grass at Norwich Airport.*

BELOW: *Sqn Ldr Dave Thomas prepares to taxi. Adopted by the city of Lincoln in 1975, PA474 is permitted to bear the coat of arms and title* City of Lincoln *in recognition of the long and deep association of the Lancaster and RAF Bomber Command with the city and its surrounding area.*

ABOVE: *Merlins stilled.*

RIGHT: *One for the fighter boys.* City of Lincoln *displaying at North Weald.*

ABOVE: *Bad weather ahead?*

RIGHT:
*Setting out
at dusk.*

During the winter of 1995–6, PA474 received a brand-new main spar which will extend her life. City of Lincoln is limited to seventy-five hours' flying time each year. Every six years the Lancaster undergoes major servicing and at this time receives a change of colour scheme and markings. In 1990 PA474 received the markings of W4964 WS-J-for-Johnnie, a famous 9 Squadron aircraft which flew its 100th operation on 15 September 1944 when 9 and 617 Squadrons made the first attack on the *Tirpitz* from Russia. After dropping its 12,000lb Tallboy, Flt Lt Doug Melrose and his crew returned to Bardney to receive a well-earned crate of whisky. J-Johnnie's nose art decorations included three 'wound stripes' – one for a 50 x 4lb incendiary container which passed through its wing. *Johnny Walker* flew 106 operational sorties by war's end. It was scrapped in 1949.

LEFT AND BELOW: *Merv Counter powering* Mickey the Moocher *over Lincolnshire and out over the coast near Skegness before skirting the North Sea and displaying at Louth. The lively Lanc certainly gave us a run for our money!*

DESMOND DAK

The bomb which blasted thousands into glory
Was the greatest war invention, goes the story,
Or the Radar, which revealed in darkest skies
Location of each little plane that flies;
But beleaguered man's invention, blest to Heaven,
Was the Dak, the DC Three – C Forty-Seven

'C Forty-Seven' by Jasper Miles

ABOVE: *ZA947 continues to be the workhorse of the BBMF, participating in displays both in the UK (as here, at Old Warden on 4 July 1999, being waved off by the 'GIs') and on the Continent, as well as fulfilling its normal tasks of crew training and support (it keeps the pilots of the Lancaster current during the winter months when the bomber is out of action).*

LEFT: *Manufactured in March 1942, ZA947 was adopted by Strike Command and issued to the BBMF in March 1993. In 1998, during a minor servicing with Air Atlantique at Coventry, ZA947's markings were changed from Flt Lt David Lord's aircraft (YS-DM) to YS-H of 77 Squadron from Fassberg in Germany.*

TO THE MEN WHO TURNED THE SPANNER

To the men who turned the spanner,
to the men who pulled the wrench,
To the men who did refuelling
with the octane's heavy stench,
To the 'genius' with radar,
to the man who fixed the gun,
To the service crews in freezing cold
when working was not fun,
To those who brought the bombs along
and loaded them aboard,
To the artist of the mascot
be it Pluto or a broad,
To the cooks who cooked the dinner,
though not always cordon bleu,
To the girl who brought the break truck
(and what you thought of her),
To those who spread the bullshit
from their office in the warm,
To those who crewed the ambulance
in case you came to harm,
For each and every flyer
owes a debt he cannot pay.
To those who worked upon the ground
and sent him on his way.

'Cheers (A Flyer's Toast)'
by Jasper Miles, a Lancaster gunner

FACING PAGE: *Jnr Tech Ollie Moore, an engine technician, attends to the Merlin engine of Hurricane IIC LF363 at RAF Coningsby. The BBMF's six engine technicians were kept very busy with Merlin engine problems throughout the previous season when the two Hurricanes were largely unable to fly.*

ABOVE: *Sgt Keith Brenchley (left) since September 1992 Engine Trade Manager on the BBMF, and a fellow engine technician, look on as Hurricane IIC PZ865 runs up its Merlin engine at RAF Coningsby.*

RIGHT: *'In the stores, in the stores . . .'*

THEIR FINEST HOUR – WELL, TWO ACTUALLY

'. . . . Let us therefore brace ourselves to our duties, and so bear ourselves that, if the British Empire and its Commonwealth last for a thousand years, men will still say, "This was their finest hour."'

Prime Minister Winston S. Churchill, 18 June 1940

PREVIOUS PAGE: *Ready for the off from IWM Duxford to Norwich Airport on 13 September 1999 for the BoB flypast over the city. Sqn Ldr Dave Thomas, Bomber Leader, in the captain's seat, and Flt Lt Merv Counter, in the 2nd dicky's seat, go through their pre-flight check as Flt Lt Garry Simm, navigator, and Sergeant 'Ernie' Wise, flight engineer, carry out their duties.*

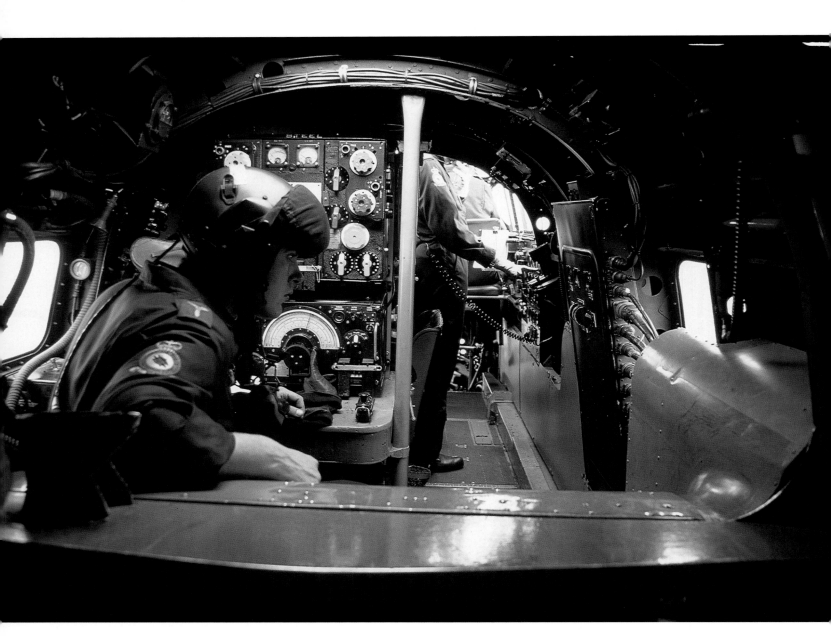

ABOVE: *Radio check. The original radio equipment is no longer in use, replaced by modern VHF/UHF radios operated by the navigator, but the wartime equipment is retained to add authenticity.*

ABOVE: *What to do? Take the mid-upper turret, or the tail? An excellent compromise was reached when Sgt 'Sid' Siddell became 'rear gunner' with one of my cameras and I took the mid-upper with my other camera, mainly because this turret offers a 360° view of the Lanc and beyond. 'Shiney', meanwhile, has taxied PS915 out and will join us after take-off.*

RIGHT: *A Frazer Nash Mk 150 mid-upper gun turret was discovered at a gunnery school in Argentina (it had never been fitted to an aircraft) and was brought to Britain aboard HMS Hampshire in 1973 and installed in PA474 in 1975.*

ABOVE: *Good old 'Sid'. Spot-on suggesting that once in the mid-upper, lift one's bottom from the leather strap, turn 180° and face the rear for an unobstructed view. To turn the turret, put your arm behind your back and feel for the turning knob. Forget to lock it and you'll have that spinning feeling!*

RIGHT: *I thought it was the Lancaster that was supposed to 'corkscrew'!*

ABOVE: *Sqn Ldr Simmons slips 'the surly bonds of Earth' to tuck in tighter.*

LEFT: *'Sid' draws a bead! Sgt (now Chief Tech) John Siddle is an airframe technician who joined the BBMF as airframe trade manager in 1998. Since joining the RAF in 1977, 'Sid' has worked on nine different types of aircraft in the RAF.*
('Sid' Siddell)

ABOVE: *'Shiney' comes in closer as 'Sid' rotates the tail turret for a better angle.*

('Sid' Siddell)

RIGHT: *Time to break away.*

ABOVE: *OK, you asked for it! 'Shiney' pulls in tight as we head over the Broads for Norwich and the BoB flypast.*
('Sid' Siddell)

RIGHT: *High noon. The outskirts of Norwich loom large as the pair head for City Hall on the stroke of twelve.*
('Sid' Siddell)

ABOVE: *Boyhood dream come true. Over my home city in a Lanc, on Battle of Britain Day! Below, the good citizens of Norwich must be looking skyward as we converge on Thorpe railway station off Prince of Wales Road (centre). Carrow Road, Norwich City's stadium, is at the top.*

LEFT: *'Sid''s sensational shot! Rear gunner's-eye view over City Hall with the RAF parade in progress out front. 'Sid' should get a gong for this one!*

('Sid' Siddell)

RIGHT: *A tale of two cities. With the Spitfire's wings looking like a canard,* City of Lincoln *and PS915 overfly Norwich, passing the Norman cathedral and castle keep below. The city was devastated in the series of Baedeker raids in 1942, rebuilt, and to this day retains the proud heritage associated with the BBMF gained during many years when the Flight was stationed at RAF Coltishall nearby.*

BELOW: *Come rain, come shine. As dusk approaches PA474 and PS915 head for home bathed in the evening sun, but not before Norwich Airport gets its flyby.*

City of Lincoln *at Norwich Airport after the BoB flypast: Sqn Ldr Dave Thomas (left), 'Shiney' Simmons (centre) and (right) Flt Lt Garry Simm, Lancaster navigator. A former Vulcan display pilot, Dave Thomas is a multi-engine pilot instructor on Jetstreams at Cranwell. This was Dave's third and final full season on the Flight. 'Shiney' joined the RAF in 1975 and flew the F.-4 Phantom prior to becoming a QFI. Since 1986 he has flown the Tornado F.2 and is an instructor with 56(R) Squadron. He has over 2,700 hours on the Tornado and 5,000 hours' total flying time. Garry Simm, on his first season with the BBMF, joined the RAF as a navigator in 1980 and is an instructor on the Tornado OCU with 56(R) Squadron at Coningsby.*

ABOVE: *There can be no finer sight than to see a Lanc and a Spitfire this close.*

RIGHT: *Brothers in arms. PA474 and PS915 skirt Attlebridge airfield, the US 466th BG B-24 Liberator base from 1944 to 1945. Nearby is another ex-B-24 base, at Shipdham, where, on the night of 3/4 November 1943, Lancaster III LM360 O-Oboe of 61 Squadron, piloted by Flt Lt William 'Bill' Reid RAFVR, crash-landed returning from Düsseldorf. Before the target was reached Reid's Lancaster had been crippled by two separate fighter attacks which wounded him and members of his crew, and killed his navigator. Despite severe injuries Reid carried on to the target, where he released his bombs. The wireless operator, badly wounded, died in hospital. It was while convalescing that Reid was told he had been awarded the Victoria Cross. No fewer than ten VCs were awarded to Lancaster aircrew.*

ABOVE: *Griffon to the fore.*

RIGHT: *High flight!*

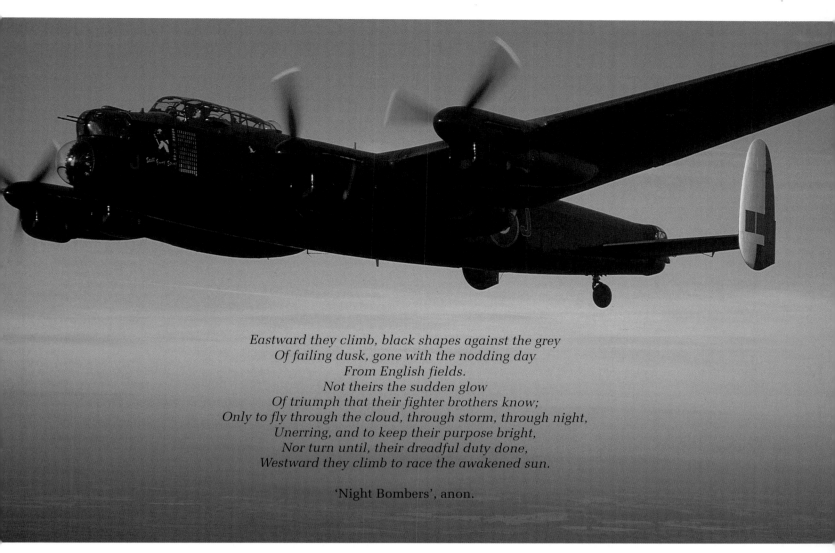

Eastward they climb, black shapes against the grey
Of failing dusk, gone with the nodding day
From English fields.
Not theirs the sudden glow
Of triumph that their fighter brothers know;
Only to fly through the cloud, through storm, through night,
Unerring, and to keep their purpose bright,
Nor turn until, their dreadful duty done,
Westward they climb to race the awakened sun.

'Night Bombers', anon.

Oh! I have slipped the surly bonds of Earth
And danced the skies on laughter-silvered wings;
Sunward I've climbed, and joined the tumbling mirth
Of sun-split clouds – and done a hundred things . . .

'Shiney', smiling for the camera, often recites this famous poem, 'High Flight' by Plt Off John Gillespie Magee, a nineteen-year-old American Spitfire pilot of 41 'Falcon' Squadron RCAF, who was killed in a mid-air collision on 11 December 1941. He is buried at Scopwick, Lincolnshire.

Over and out!

JOURNEY MADE, DUTY DONE

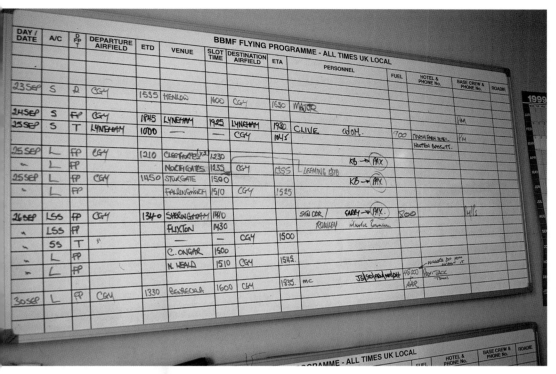

A biting wind, a searing frost,
A dome of cloud, a misty moon,
Below, a flaming holocaust,
The engines' heavy droning tune.
The spiteful deadly beads of flak
That weave a pattern on the night,
The searchlight cones across the
    black,
A piercing, vicious blinding white,
The aircraft jinking as it tries
To keep its course and yet evade
The fighters, swarming thick as flies,
That try to stem this cavalcade,
This endless wave, this marathon
Of vengeful bombers, dim and black,
Their crews, relentless, pressing on
To seek, to find and to attack.
A burning bomber hurtling down,
A blazing pyre across the sky,
The incandescence of a town
Alight with flares, prepared to die.
A voice upon the intercom,
The sudden chattering of a gun,
The fire-burst of a fallen bomb,
Its journey made, its duty done.

'Ops' by Audrey Grealy

Heading out. Supporters from the Lincolnshire Lancaster Association hug the flight line at Coningsby. Having seen the results 'Sid' achieved, I just had to get in the tail turret (feet first is the only way).

ABOVE AND BELOW: *Films in the Canons loaded for action! The machine-guns aren't! Once seated, the gunner's sliding clear-vision panel is superb for air-to-air photography, but only if the fighters fly at eye level. However, the prop wash from the Lanc's two inboard engines and turbulence caused by PA474's twin tail force the fighters to fly low, so an upright, out-of-seat experience with knees slightly bent has to be adopted so that your big bone dome clears the top and your camera is pointing through the CVP. Now, as the turret rises and falls, so too do your aching thighs! Aching arms and thigh strains in the tail are well worth it, though, when Grp Capt Peter Ruddock in XIX PS915 (leading) and Sqn Ldr Clive Rowley in XIX PM631 strike a pose like this.*

*Bad weather
near
Blakeney
Point sees
Clive Rowley
head off.*

ABOVE: *Might as well vacate the tail and head for the sharp end via the main spar and other obstacles akin to an assault course, but pausing to look out of the astrodome. Wow!*

RIGHT: City of Lincoln *goes around for another pass over Sheringham.*

ABOVE: *Grey skies have cleared up!*

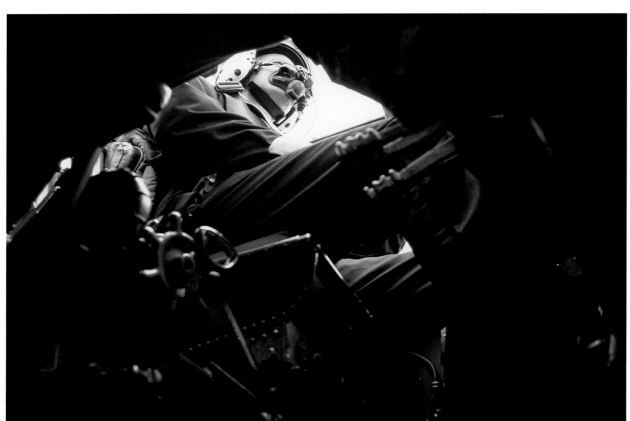

RIGHT: *New boy on the block. Merv Counter, on his first 'tour' on the Lanc, maintains course to the west of Norwich and heads for the Norfolk–Suffolk border.*

Flixton (near Bungay), Suffolk, home of the Norfolk and Suffolk Aviation Museum, which has on display, among other memorabilia, pieces of fabric saved from the fire of LF363. The site is also home to the US 446th BG, 8th AF, and Royal Observer Corps exhibitions. There is also the RAF Air Sea Rescue and Coastal Command Museum, as well as over twenty-five historic aircraft. Indoor exhibitions both civil and military, feature the pioneer years, through World War I to the present day with special displays on Boulton & Paul and World War II Decoy Sites.

LEFT: *Ship-shape and Bristol fashion. Flt Lt Rolly Hendry in the 2nd dicky's seat. Rolly, who was on his second season with the Flight, joined the RN as a helicopter pilot in 1980 before joining the RAF in 1992 as an instructor on Jetstream aircraft. He then converted to the AWACs, and is currently a pilot instructor on 23 Squadron at Waddington.*

BELOW: *A bridge too far. Passing Ipswich off to port with the Orwell river bridge in the distance.*

Shades of the Dambusters. PA474 passes over Abberton reservoir south-south-east of Colchester, Essex.

'...S.A.S.O. (Senior Air Staff Officer), has given permission for us to use the reservoirs at Uppingham* and Colchester to practise on. He has fixed up with a film studio or something to rig up a special framework on the water barrage which will make them look very like our own objectives ... From now on we are going to carry out attacks against these places using nine aircraft at a time. These attacks will begin tonight. The sort of thing I visualize is three flights of three aircraft flying in formation at night along our special route. We will reach the first lake; we will then attack singly, according to my instructions on the R.T., from exactly 60 feet and at exactly 232 miles an hour ... In the meantime, other crews are to keep their hands in with bombing a spotlight flying over the Wash. Six other special crews will be sent to another lake to carry out a special form of attack there.'
Enemy Coast Ahead *by Guy Gibson V.C., D.S.O., D.F.C.*

On the night of 16/17 May 1943 617 Squadron dropped their spinning 'bouncing' bombs on the approaches to German dams in the Ruhr. The Möhne and Eder dams were breached but a heavy, low mist shielded the Sorpe dam making accurate bombing impossible. Of the nineteen crews who set out, Operation Chastise cost eight Lancasters and their crews. Wg Cdr Guy Gibson DSO DFC was awarded the Victoria Cross for his leadership on the raid and for drawing enemy fire on his own aircraft.

*See page 36

LEFT: *Low-level in a Lanc recalls the experimental daylight raid on Augsburg, Bavaria, on 17 April 1942. AM Arthur Harris, AOC Bomber Command, wanted the MAN engine plant raided by twelve Lancasters, six each from 44 Squadron at Waddington and 97 Squadron at Woodhall Spa, flying at 500 feet and in daylight. Six Lancs and thirty-seven aircrew were lost on the operation, of which twelve were made PoW, including Sqn Ldr J. S. Sherwood DFC*, who was recommended for a VC by Harris and was awarded the DSO. Eight officers were awarded the DFC. Sqn Ldr John Deering Nettleton, a South African, who led the operation, was awarded the VC. (As CO of 44 Squadron, Wg Cdr Nettleton FTR from Turin, 12/13 July 1943.)*

RIGHT: *Men in black. Sqn Ldr Andy Marson, navigator, on his first season with the Flight, is a navigation instructor flying Dominies, while Sgt Ernie Wise, 'Eng', on his second year with the BBMF, is an air engineer instructor at Cranwell. Operational requirements on this flight dictated that two navigators were part of the crew (because Andy Marson was not current on Lancs) so Squadron Leader Brian Clark, on his fifth season with the BBMF, filled the first navigator position. 'Brain' joined the RN in 1965 as a fast jet Observer (Navigation). During his 12 years with the 'dark blues', he flew Sea Vixens from HMS Hermes and Eagle and F4 Phantoms from HMS Ark Royal. In 1980 he joined the RAF as a Navigator, where he spent 9 years on the Phantom, including six years as an instructor, followed by a Flight Commander tour in Germany. Brian converted to the Tornado F3 in 1989 and is currently engaged as an F3 Simulator Instructor. The navigator's station is rarely used in flight apart from on long legs to displays on the Continent, the Channel Isles, and to Benbecula. He stands behind the captain with map and stop-watch, while the 'Eng', who is responsible for fuel management of the aircraft, stands or crouches, because of the close proximity of the nav table, to maintain a watch on the flight engineer's panel (right).*

After a flypast at a church at Chipping Ongar to the east of North Weald, PA474 made three exciting runs over the airfield to provide the appreciative crowd with several topside views of the aircraft. The ex-WW2 Lanc pilot beside me in the nose had seen it all before, having survived fifty-seven ops on 61 Squadron in twelve different Lancs – all of them shot down before war's end.

Best place to be: looking down on the M25/M11 junction through the Mk XIV stabilised bomb-sight.

FACING PAGE: *Me and my shadow!*

RIGHT: *Two thousand feet over Lakenheath.*

BELOW: *'Coningsby's socked in, chaps – round again!'*

Finals. Journey made, duty done.

Tail-end Charlie. PA474 is fitted with a Frazer Nash Mk 121 tail-turret without its original Village Inn gun-laying radar. Cartridge-case ejection chutes are still fitted, and to make the aircraft even more authentic a wind deflector of wood and fabric construction was added in the winter of 1985. Note the badge of the Air Gunners' Association, whose motto is VIGILANTIA ET VIRTUTE (and 'We aim never to please'!)

(Dale Featherby)

MICKEY THE MOOCHER

Lancaster *City of Lincoln*'s markings changed in February 2000, when PA474 adopted the markings of B3 EE176 QR-M *Mickey the Moocher* of 61 Squadron at Skellingthorpe. Paint for the new scheme is satin-finish. In addition, the bomb-bay doors were changed to their original configuration. M-Mike finished the war with 115 ops recorded on its bomb log on the nose, but official records show Mickey completing 128 ops before it was retired to become a ground instructional airframe.

One of the pilots who flew the original *Mickey the Moocher* is Australian Frank Mouritz. 'My crew and I arrived at 61 Squadron, Skellingthorpe, Lincolnshire, from 5 FLS Syerston nearby, on the morning of 27 September 1944. I carried out my first operation that night. It was a six-and-a-half-hour trip to Kaiserslautern with Flt Lt King and crew. I was an observer and had no duties except to gain experience. The trip was uneventful and I was really amazed at the target with the sheer brilliance of searchlights and explosions of bombs, flak and photo flashes. The biggest fireworks display I have ever seen was nothing compared to the target.

'During the next ten days or so we carried out our first two operations: one to Wilhelmshaven and one to Bremen, in QR-8. We were then allocated a permanent aircraft – QR-M – with the nose art of *Mickey the Moocher*, a real veteran with 119 trips on the nose. It was quite something to have our own plane, another milestone in our air force career. The ground crew were very proud of their plane and the number of trips completed. This showed good maintenance and a lot of luck. We hoped that the luck had not all been used up as it was usually considered that to survive a tour required about seventy-five per cent luck and twenty-five per cent skill.

'By this time *Mickey* was nearly worn out. The four engines were close to the hours for a complete change, the controls were sloppy, and

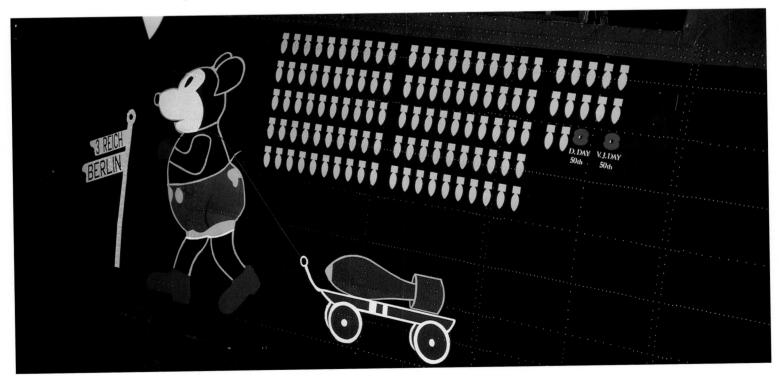

Mickey Rides Again! Resplendent in its new black satin finish, PA474 has now adopted the markings of QR-M, the famous 61 Squadron 'kite'. During the war operational aircraft like the Lancaster were painted black underneath to make them difficult for the enemy to see at night. Ironically, both the two DH Chipmunks operated by the Flight are now in all-black also.

Wing and a prayer. Mickey's nose-art captured on camera while perching precariously on the edge.

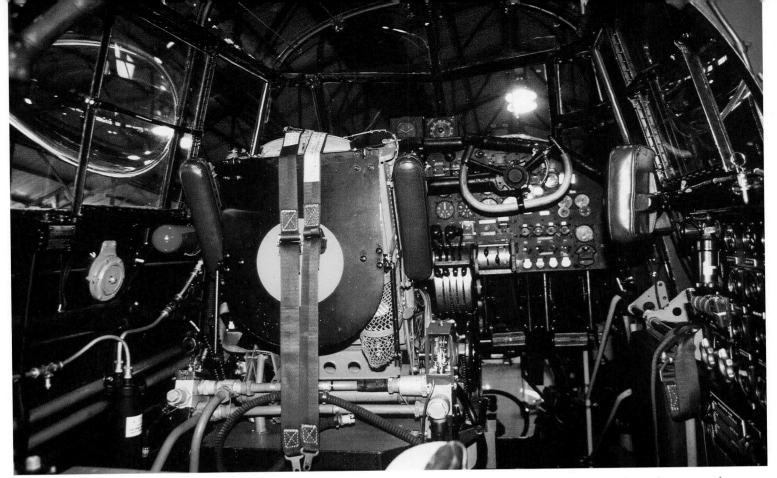

*'Heady Metal'. A Lanc cockpit has that uniquely British atmosphere of alluring instrumentation, unfussy but rugged construction, and the intoxicating scent of past glories which places it on a par with the finest Rollers, veteran Jags and vintage MGs (*with black labrador of course*).*

she had dozens of patches on wings and fuselage. She took a lot of runway to get off the ground with a full load of fuel and bombs. We were the new crew given the oldest Lanc on the squadron, but we were proud of her.

'She took us on our first trip on 5 October, a daylight one to the Dutch coast, with a fighter escort, to bomb sea walls (dykes) in an attempt to flood German artillery batteries that were holding up the advance of the British ground forces. The raid was not successful, although we bombed from low level.

'At this stage I could sense through *Mickey* the feelings of all the crews that had survived over 100 trips in this special aircraft, passing on their experience and good luck for a successful tour, a sort of feeling of comradeship and well-being which is

hard to describe. *Mickey* was something to look up to, a guiding star. I get a similar feeling now, when, as a bushwalking guide, I lead a group of walkers through our magnificent Karri forests.

'Our next trip, on the night of 14/15 October, was a seven-and-a-half-hour night flight to Brunswick with 233 Lancs and seven Mosquitoes. This was an area attack with Cookies and incendiaries. A large amount of damage was inflicted. This was also a milestone as 15 October was my twenty-first birthday, and we had our first fighter combat. This is recorded in the debriefing combat report, as follows: "Nearing the target area the mid-upper gunner [Arthur Bass] spotted a fighter approaching from the port quarter above which then appeared

to side-slip into position behind them. He ordered the pilot to corkscrew as he opened fire, while also giving the rear gunner [Den Cluett] the fighter's position and who, upon seeing it too, also opened fire. The fighter dived quickly away, the mid-upper gunner giving it a final burst as it disappeared out of range."

'The next trip, on 19 October, was another good one: seven hours to Nuremberg with 263 Lancs and seven Mosquitoes, again area bombing with a large number of casualties and damage inflicted. We were beginning to get a little confident now with Laurie Cooper, our navigator, keeping us on time and track and in the middle of the stream, and Pete Smith, our bomb-aimer, directing the bombing run with precision. And we were obtaining good target photos.

Setting sun, setting course for home ('Sid' Siddell)

'Our next trip, on 23 October, was another daylight one to the Dutch coast to attack the same batteries as before. It was also unsuccessful.

'*Mickey* took us for her 130th and last operation on 6 November, to bomb the Mitteland Canal at Gravenhorst. The marking force had difficulty in finding the target due to low cloud. We were called down to bomb at low level and I recall selecting full flap and wheels down to enable us to lose height in time. The first markers were so accurate that they fell in the canal and were extinguished. We were one of the few Lancs that bombed before the Master Bomber abandoned the raid due to low cloud.

'On 9 November we flew *Mickey* to Netheravon, a one-and-a-half-hour flight from Skellingthorpe, and returned in QR-F piloted by Flg Off Burns. *Mickey* must have been retired from operations now because, along with a Halifax and a Stirling, she was to be loaded with Red Cross parcels to ascertain the number that could be carried during relief flights for the liberated Allied PoWs on the continent.

'*Mickey* remained at Netheravon until 30 November, when we travelled in a Lancaster piloted by Flt Lt Greenfield, to fly her back to Skellingthorpe. Some other crew must have flown her away to 1653 CU after this as possibly we were on leave.

'We were allocated our new QR-M in early December. What a difference to fly! When doing our first air test with no bombs and limited fuel, I opened the throttle on take-off and we were flung back in our seats. She behaved like a sports car.

'We had by now completed twelve trips and flew the new *Mickey* (although no art was ever painted on the nose) to the end of our tour, except for a few weeks in January and February 1945 when she was being repaired after getting shot up and having a dicey landing.

'I returned to Australia in July with the probability of starting a second tour as part of Tiger Force, the new name of 5 Group, bombing Japan. The atom bomb prevented this.'

'M for Merv'.

'Merv the Swerve'. Flt Lt Merv Counter and Sqn Ldr Stu Reid put Mickey through its paces while Sqn Ldr Andy Marson, navigator, and Sgt Phil McConville, air engineer, 'stand to' behind their seats.

'Beat ya to the beach!'

Oft this earth I leave behind,
And soar God's heavens.
Till sun and stars I find,
And fence the towering clouds
With others of my kind.
Fear not if I should lose my way,
Nor keep sad hearts
For my returning day.
'Tis that I flew the heavens too high
And reached God's guiding hand,
And heard him answer to my cry;
'Your journey's done – now land.'

'Last Landing', written by A. Burford Sleep two days before he 'flew the heavens too high'.
A bomb-aimer on Lancasters, he was killed returning from a raid on Cologne. He had
handed copies of this poem to each other member of the crew the night of the raid, and he
was the only one killed, although others were injured and wounded. Ironically, his brother,
Sqn Ldr R. M. Sleep (109 Squadron), marked the target on Cologne that night.

Captain's Log. Squadron Leader Dave Thomas (left) counter-signs Squadron Leader Stu Reid's log book.

Thanks everyone, thank you one and all – for everything.

Bibliography and Further Reading

Bowman, Martin W. *RAF at War*. PSL.

—— & Boiten, Theo (1996) *Raiders of the Reich*. Airlife.

Day, Sqn Ldr Paul (1986). 'A Novice's Viewpoint'. *Wingspan* magazine.

Hammersley, Ronald A. DFM. *Into Battle with 57 Squadron*.

Leach, Sqn Ldr R. E. BA RAF (Lincolnshire Lancaster Committee) *A Lancaster at Peace*.

Leaf, Edward (1997) *Above All Unseen: The RAF's PR Units 1939–45*. PSL.

Miles, Jasper. *Echoes: A Tribute in Verse*.

Richards, Denis (1974) RAF 1939–45. *Vol. 1: The Fight at Odds*. HMSO.

Shores, Christopher & Clive Williams (1994) *Aces High: A Tribute to the Most Notable Fighter Pilots of the British and Commonwealth Air Forces in WWII*. London: Grub Street.